MiSTAKES MEN MAKE

MISTAKES MEN MAKE

**You're a man.
You're a mess.
You need all the
help you can get.**

DANIEL BILLETT

BLOOMSBURY

First US and Canadian Edition 2007

Conceived and produced by
Elwin Street Limited
144 Liverpool Road
London N1 1LA
United Kingdom
www.elwinstreet.com

Published by Bloomsbury USA, New York
Distributed to the trade by Holtzbrinck Publishers

A catalog record for this book is available from the Library of Congress.

ISBN-10 1-59691-423-8
ISBN-13 978-1-59691-423-0

1 3 5 7 9 10 8 6 4 2

Printed in Singapore

With thanks to the following for the use of photographs:
iStockPhoto: 84
Mark Lobo: 78
Photolibrary: 2, 51, 61, 69, 72, 98, 100, 104, 118, 128
Gregory White: 75
Getty Images: all remaining photographs.

CONTENTS

INTRODUCTION

Let's face it, men, some of us would be happier if society would let us wear the clothes our primitive forebears wore thousands of years ago. Skins and a club, maybe, or perhaps a sackcloth robe and sandals. As for the effort of keeping hair and beard clean and trimmed, it's just a waste of energy, right?

But the ramshackle charm of centuries long past, wearing any old clothes any old how and growing hair in all kinds of places, can no longer cut it in a world where the weight of the mammoth you killed is no longer an accurate measure of manhood; it is no longer acceptable not to make an effort.

But there is, of course, another side to the male specimen: his vanity, and it too is as ancient and as vast as the rivers of olive oil that Homer's victorious warriors used to soften their skin and hair. Man preens: for women, for one another, and particularly for himself. And, sad to say, the results of this are often no better. It's not enough, it seems, to make an effort—you must make the right effort.

There is a fine balance to be struck. And who is there to tell you when it has all gone horribly and tragically wrong? It is I, Daniel Billett, men's fashion oracle at About.com. Someone needs to be the arbiter, and I've decided it shall be me.

There have been many fashion crimes through the ages, from Moses' unibrow, to Caesar's kiss curl. Those great men might have been beyond my help, but you lesser mortals are redeemable.

So I will deign to impart some wisdom. Man needs to know the error of his fashion ways, and this humble little guide will be a starting-point. Herein you will find a variety of egregious fashion errors, the results of caring too little and too much about one's appearance, and a few nuggets of wisdom guaranteed to correct any "quirks" of personal style. Read on, my friends, and learn.

Swimwear and pants;
shoes and socks; shirts,
suits, and ties.

CHAPTER 1

CLOTHING

Tight swimwear, better known as the Speedo Effect or Banana Hammock, came to us courtesy of Mark Spitz in 1972. He took home seven gold medals during that year's Olympics, so we will try to forgive him.

However, unless you are an Olympic swimmer (it doesn't count if you're retired), save the skimpy swimwear for the tanning booth or a very remote beach.

The world is full of phallic symbols. Try not to create any more.

Don't get caught smuggling cucumbers. Tight pants leave nothing to the imagination, and trust me, imagination is your friend.

I say hang loose and swing free, because remember, men, not only are tight pants embarrassing, they're also linked to male infertility.

It is also possible to take this too far the other way. Remember Hammertime, when the tragically deformed offspring of the old knickerbockers came into style? Colorful, baggy, disastrous.

Bit like pajamas, really, weren't they?

How times have changed. Baggy pants are now made out of denim.

This is not, in fact, any better.

Recent baggy looks have been belted literally below the bottom, combining the worst of the voluminous, in both pants and briefs.

One should never be in danger of tripping over one's own pants—at least, not while wearing them.

Shorts can go wrong in two directions: too far up and too far down.

Short shorts: anything cut above mid-thigh reveals far more about you than most strangers (and many friends) want to know.

Long shorts: anything that hangs below the knee, and you might as well wear pants. Don't even think about wearing Capris.

Be aware that shorts provide a less interrupted view of the crotch than pants, especially when sitting. Appropriately modest underwear is recommended.

A few brief words about socks.

They should always be worn with shoes or boots.

Socks should never be a feature of your outfit, though. They should remain hidden below long trousers, or worn short around the ankles if the weather demands you wear shorts.

When Birkenstocks climbed out of their German niche sometime in the eighties, the fashion industry groaned.

Treating your feet with respect and care is one thing, wearing open-toed, tire-tread-soled sandals made from old Mercedes-Benz parts is quite another.

And if you even think of adding socks . . .

Fashionable clothing is meant to be painful for the wearer, not the observer. Just ask a Geisha.

If you feel the need to imagine something worse, there's always dress shoes and smart socks with shorts. This was the beachwear of preference for Richard Nixon and look where that got him. No-one ever caught John F. Kennedy in that get-up.

God bless the seventies and eighties, when a man could wear stacked shoes several inches deep without being thought a complete fool.

Those days are long gone. Aren't they?

Cowboy boots look great. On cowboys.
The clue, as is so often the case, is in the name.

To elaborate, if you can wear cowboy boots
while giving the impression they are genuinely of
practical use to you in your everyday line of work,
then hats off to you, buckaroo.

If, on the other hand, you're wearing cowboy
boots in the belief they make you look like Heath
Ledger, you might want to reconsider.

RHINESTONE COWBOY

My stance on cowboy boots applies also to the cowboy outfit as a whole. Once again, if you look, speak, smell, and talk like a cowboy, nobody will think twice about your attire.

If, on the other hand, you look like a city-slicker who has paid a substantial amount of money merely to look like a cowboy . . . Let's just say the Duke wouldn't approve.

Any cowboy get-up that sparkles in any way is suitable only for children's costume parties.

Ah, the shirt. Few items of clothing can produce more affection when worn well, and more distaste when not.

Maybe because modern man feels as though he's working all of the time, he's ready to jump into a leisure shirt at a moment's notice. But be warned, fashion troubles abound when a man tries to "go casual" without proper forethought.

The nineties saw a pleasing revival of the leisure shirt, brat-pack style, with a good cut and collar (and preferably a gin martini). But all too quickly, the Hawaiian shirt and its garish cousins have fought their way back into common use. What's that saying about history repeating itself? Comedy, tragedy, and then farce.

You may think that traveling abroad, far from the censorious eyes of anybody who actually knows you, entitles you to dress in Technicolor. That's the only possible excuse for wearing a Hawaiian shirt. It's also, clearly, nonsense.

Oh, and by the way, those big flowers aren't hiding your sagging belly, and you're not going to get "lei'd" in that shirt.

The few insults that cannot be heaped upon the Hawaiian shirt are merely held in reserve for the glittery shirt. It is beneath contempt.

Perhaps it's a childish attempt to mesmerize your prey. Maybe a gold front tooth could work similarly? Or—and this is a daring suggestion—you could fall back on the old standby of scintillating conversation.

Until recently, ties were for covering the buttons on your shirt, and lending an air of silken nobility to even the most odious middle-manager. Not any more.

Ties have become as dull and witless as the corporate meetings to which they are worn. However, any attempt to inject mirth into proceedings by sporting a "novelty" tie is doomed to failure.

There are more effective ways of getting noticed, like nailing a presentation, or coming up with a plan that saves your company hundreds of thousands of dollars. Leave the novelty ties at home and get back to work.

Mickey Mouse tie? Hawaiian hula girls?
Neon coloring? All wrong.
Naked lady tie? Criminal.

If you really can't tell the difference between
an elegant tie and a pin-up girl, then you can't
go wrong with just a crisp white shirt and a
smart blazer.

A few further warnings about suits and ties: unless
you want to look like a lounge singer, avoid large
stripes; and unless you want to look like a used-car
salesman, avoid loud checks. Simple, no?

The mysteries of the bow tie are not to be dabbled
in by the uninitiated. If in doubt, go without.

If you must wear one, avoid short-sleeved shirts,
or you'll risk being mistaken for a hotel porter.

Androgyny, thy name is tracksuit: matching top, matching bottom, racing stripes, hideous. And if you and your wife have matching tracksuits, you are just asking for trouble.

In fact, any sort of his-and-hers clothing is an absolute no-no, unless you enjoy looking as though you and your not-so-better half are participating in mixed doubles at tennis.

Is it that, after a few too many, you need to match clothing to make sure you're going home with the right person? If that is the case, the drinking problem may precede the fashion problem. My advice is to seek help for both.

Inclement weather is no excuse for deplorable fashion sense. It is therefore shocking that the anorak has been permitted to replace the eminently workable—not to mention elegant—raincoat and hat combination.

Adding what amounts to a windsock to your jacket, by unfolding the hood, just compounds the matter.

"But how shall I stop myself getting wet without my beloved plastic jacket?" you ask.
I suggest an umbrella.

A certain amount of discomfort or dampness may have to be endured. This is the small price we pay for not looking shrink-wrapped.

Bling, bags, hats,
and sunglasses.

CHAPTER 2

Instead of flint axes and wooden spears,
modern man carries cell phones and legal files.

You can bet the trendy caveman had a
leather holster for his flint ax. And you can bet it
looked awful.

Even in the most beautiful suit, you will look
thoroughly unkempt carrying a plastic bag
or battered rucksack.

The golden rule for any fashion statement: quantity never equals quality. Neither, in the case of jewelry, does weight.

If the bling begins to make your neck ache, or you break out in a sweat during the layering of the karats, you are well past the sacred threshold of the fashionable.

The key word here is "subtlety."

Jewel-encrusted car logos worn between the pecs are not subtle. Neither are diamond-capped dentures.

Eventually, all good fashion choices are massacred by excess. Or by some guy named Lil Jon.

Rappers that fail to take notice of this often find themselves, sartorially speaking, on thin ice ice, baby.

Necklaces can be sexy on men, but when it comes to jewelry, less is very definitely more. Any chain that could feasibly be used to tow your car is entirely unsuitable for fashion.

David Beckham and Justin Timberlake can get away with diamond earrings, by virtue of being immensely rich, extremely popular, and devastatingly good-looking. Unless you fit all three of these categories, you can't.

The ring has a rich history of symbolism dating back throughout human history. Even now it can mark important moments in a man's life, like his wedding or his graduation. That is, however, as far as it should go.

More than two rings per hand suggests you don't know how to shop. More than two rings per finger suggests you don't know how to stop.

Any ring that interferes with the natural movement of your fingers should be discarded.

FAILED GANGSTA

While it's easy to mock heavy bling, even I am forced to concede that it has its own place in the urban culture from which it originates. Far be it even from one as fashion-savvy as I to criticize.

Pretension, however, is always worthy of criticism, and if you don't have the credentials to support your "gangsta" image, you're in serious danger of looking like an idiot.

So, if you can't rap or pimp a ride, then dressing, speaking, or accessorizing as though you can will expose you to justifiable ridicule, homey.

Man has had a long and beautiful relationship—marriage, even—with his hat. They are currently going through a rocky patch, but I for one am confident things will work themselves out.

At one time, a man's hat was as essential as his car or dog—a distinguishing and defining characteristic that he was never without. The hat was his most beloved accessory, and came with a host of styles and mores of its own.

Now, we have the baseball cap, the hat's younger, less formal sister, with whom Man is conducting an unseemly affair.

Just remember, she is a cap, not a hat—remember the love and affection Man felt for his hat in the old days, and for goodness' sake, don't throw it all away for a cheap fling.

That said, as in any relationship, there are a few rules to obey: stick to classic, sober colors, and styles that flatter rather than obscure the shape of your face. Oh, and never wear a hat indoors.

If even these simple requirements elude you, then you clearly don't deserve her and should remain doomed to bare-headed inelegance.

Sunglasses should only be worn in the sun—again, the clue is in the name.

You essentially have two options. There's cool: think Arnold Schwarzenegger in *The Terminator*, or Will Smith in *Men in Black*.

And then there is not so cool. Big, bug-eyed sunglasses reminiscent of the seventies and early eighties have unfortunately made their way back into "fashion," the "alien-insect-invader" look being suddenly, and briefly I am sure, desirable.

Those eyeglasses that turn into sunglasses when you walk outside are very weird indeed. They are, however, infinitely preferable to "clip-on" sunglasses.

Spectacles are a way of life for many men. This is not an excuse—in fact, it's all the more reason to make sure they look good on you. Vast lenses and thick frames are best kept for the chemistry lab.

With glasses and sunglasses, the shape of the frame should compliment your face. Bring this book with you to the eyeglass store—the sales assistant will help you out. If necessary, take someone you trust with you when shopping for frames.

Hair, facial hair,
and body hair.

CHAPTER 3

HAIR

Some of these guys look in the mirror before heading out for the day and say to themselves, "Damn, I look good." They are delusional. Or victims of a mad experimental hairstylist.

The ponytail is a non-hairstyle. On no account grow one if you are a computer programmer— some stereotypes are best left unfulfilled.

Very few men wear dreadlocks well.

None of them is white.

Genetics is one thing. Negligence is another. It's permissible to have bad hair because you're going bald. It's not permissible to have bad hair because you just haven't made an effort.

Having said that, it is perfectly possible to look good with thinning hair.

It is impossible to look good if you're desperately trying to conceal your thinning hair.

If you're thinning on top, wearing your hair long at the back and sides suggests aging hippy or cult member.

The comb-over fools no-one. It does, however, make the wearer look a fool. Its most celebrated advocate is Donald Trump. Need I say more?

The toupee is a moral conundrum. If you've ever seen a good one, how would you know? If you've ever seen a bad one, you'll know why the good ones are so expensive. After much deliberation I have decided to condemn it on the grounds of its inherent dishonesty. Plus you might need to be outside on a windy day at some point.

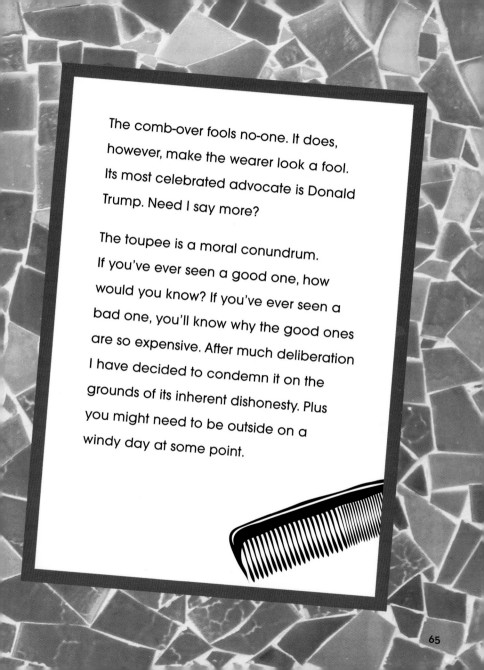

Golden rule for going bald gracefully:

Shave your head.

Enough said.

Many famous and distinguished men have worn facial hair: Confucius, Jesus Christ, Santa Claus, William Shakespeare, and Abraham Lincoln, to name just a few. They all had other things going for them.

Exotic facial hair may be an attempt to appear creative or unique. Such attempts almost inevitably fail.

Long, shaggy beard? Looks great. On Gandalf.

Sideburns were originally grown to protect a rifleman's cheeks from powder burns when using a flintlock musket.

How often do you use a flintlock musket?

OK, you can grow them. But no lower than your earlobe.

Partial facial hair is risky. The risk being you might decide to wear it.

The goatee and the soul patch are relics of the nineties. Let them rest in peace.

Thick mustache: we're not part of the Colonies any more.

Thin mustache: just creepy.

Toothbrush mustache: here's looking at you, Adolf.

Stubble is acceptable if you're good-looking, and not intending to kiss anyone.

If you must have facial hair, wear a full beard, neatly cropped.

Any facial hair that can trap food must be instantly and mercilessly razed.

ELVIS WANNABE

A few points on the inadvisability of
attempting to look like the King:

Any hairstyle that doubles as a sunshade
is to be avoided.

Any facial hair that risks engulfing your ears, ditto.

Elvis was plagued by stalkers, ill-health,
drug addiction, and, if the internet is to be
believed, UFOs. Do you really want to follow
in these footsteps?

Remember back in the seventies and eighties when Tom Selleck and Burt Reynolds were hot properties? Well, I am happy to say that times have changed. For starters, Mankind has made massive advances in hair-removal technology.

Putting a man on the Moon was nothing compared to the invention of electrolysis.

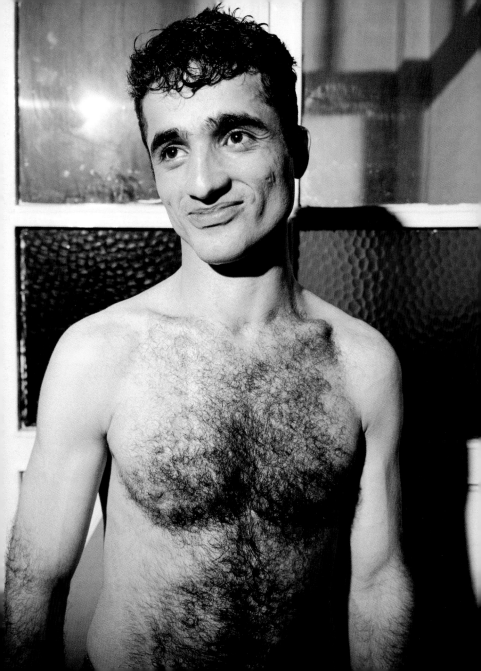

Given these massive advances, it's a shock to see the occasional Sasquatch sporting a Speedo at the pool or beach.

Think of the children!

Body hair is totally useless to us as a species; evolution is phasing it out for a reason. Consider giving Mother Nature a helping hand—waxing isn't as bad as they make it out to be.

OK, it is. But it's still better than looking like an extra from *Planet of the Apes*.

Ear and nose tufts, by the way, indicate a total lack of self-respect.

Acceptable places to cultivate hair: head;
armpits; chest, arms, and legs within reason;
pubic regions.

Unacceptable places to cultivate hair:
everywhere else.

Personal hygiene, physique,
and ornamentation.

CHAPTER 4

Wearing clothes from the dirty hamper, or finding something under the bed that should have been washed four workouts ago, is pure sloth (one of the Seven Deadly Sins, in case you need reminding. Pride is another, but we'll gloss over that.) Hardly a recipe for success, romantic or professional.

I can only assume wearing dirty clothes is the result of chronic low self-esteem, in which case you might try therapy. After all, there's no sense compounding a funk with a funky odor.

Nails are not to be chewed. If you need more roughage in your diet, try popcorn or oats. The cuticle is not a food group.

Stressed out? Try worry beads.

Excess energy? Bounce that foot or go for a run.

Man-icures are not just for the fairer sex—the word itself should encourage you.

A brief story about Michael Jordan, for further reassurance: when he first started getting manicures, salons everywhere were suddenly full of seven-foot tall men emulating their idol.

Don't be afraid to slip into one of these nail places yourself. No blushing. Just act like you have been there before.

Having said that, if they offer to apply nail polish, run.

Toenails are also in need of regular maintenance, not least because ingrowing ones are surprisingly painful.

Hint: cut them flat across the top, if you haven't graduated to the salon yet.

Despite the example of the yogic masters, chewing your toenails is out of the question. A pedicure is far more hygienic, not to mention easier on the spine.

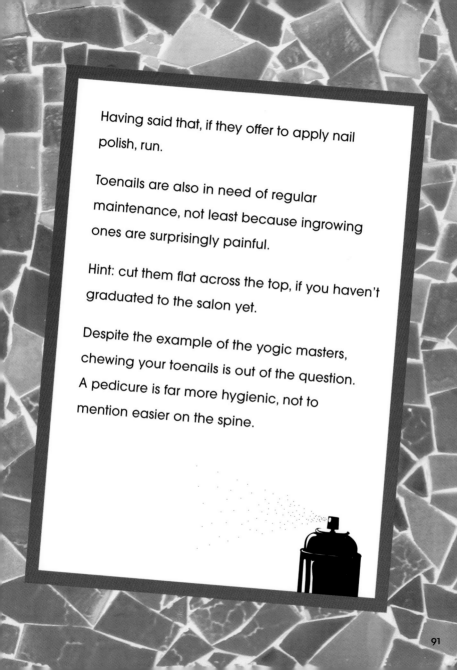

If you have a genuine problem with overactive sweat glands, wear a plain white t-shirt under your dress shirt. It'll soak up the sweat so that less of it comes through to create those embarrassing damp patches.

Men shouldn't have breasts. Owners of male mammaries often blame this unfortunate occurrence on the growth hormones found in dairy and meat products—modern man, apparently, puts out less testosterone than his leaner forebears.

I'm more inclined to blame it on powered lawnmowers and desk jobs.

If you believe the hormone argument, there is surgery. If you believe me, try bench presses. Trust me, my way is cheaper and far less painful.

Tan lines around the swimsuit area are, I am reliably informed, sexy and justifiable. Tan lines elsewhere are something of a minefield. The piebald look isn't in right now, so make a little effort to roast yourself evenly.

Mind you, given that sun exposure is a primary cause of skin cancer, you might consider forgoing the tan altogether. Between you and me, a good quality, subtle fake tan is a worthy investment.

A fake tan that makes you look orange, however, is not.

Multiple piercings are another fashion choice that baffles your oracle.

I find the "intimate" ones particularly puzzling. Call me narrow-minded, but my little oracle is quite happy the way he is, thank you.

The phrase "infection waiting to happen" seems particularly apposite here.

Tattoos: another link with our Stone Age past. That mummy they found on glacier in the European Alps a while back, deep frozen for 4000 years—he had a tattoo, believe it or not.

Some of us have come a long way in 4000 years. Some less so. Once a sign of brotherhood amongst bikers and sailors, the tattoo has suddenly turned into a fashion accessory.

Again your oracle pleads for common sense. Surely the dangers of hepatitis and misspellings should put you off. Failing that, consider the gray blur your tattoo will become when age begins to take its toll . . .

Final note on tattoos: remember Johnny Depp's "Winona Forever?" Forever never lasting quite as long as we imagine, it now reads "Winos Forever."

Laser removal is painful. If you must have a tattoo, best avoid the names, no?

AGING PUNK ROCKER

Ah, rebellious youth. Very droll. The problem arises when you hit rebellious middle- or old-age. Sagging piercings and blurred tattoos really don't inspire the same lust they did when you first had them done. And leather trousers are rather less flattering with the onset of middle-age spread.

The mummified, yet miraculously still breathing, bodies of The Rolling Stones should be ample warning to you.

Posture and playing—
with yourself, and with
others.

CHAPTER 5

BODY
LANGUAGE

Contrary to popular belief, your testicles will not suffocate if you sit with your knees less than six inches apart.

The legs-akimbo pose suggests a slightly desperate desire to demonstrate one's masculinity—and total lack of regard for etiquette, especially on mass transport.

It's possibly some sort of primal mating ritual— apes at the zoo can be observed adopting a similar pose. Men and primates . . . Well, be thankful at least one of them wears pants.

The ape or monkey is, in fact, a very useful guide to body language unsuitable for a man.

Knuckle-dragging walk? Check.

Inappropriate lack of inhibition with regard to bodily functions? Check.

Unregulated growth of body hair? Check.

Spend a little time at the zoo, and any of your own personal habits that you spot imitated by the apes, make a note to cut them ruthlessly out of your lifestyle.

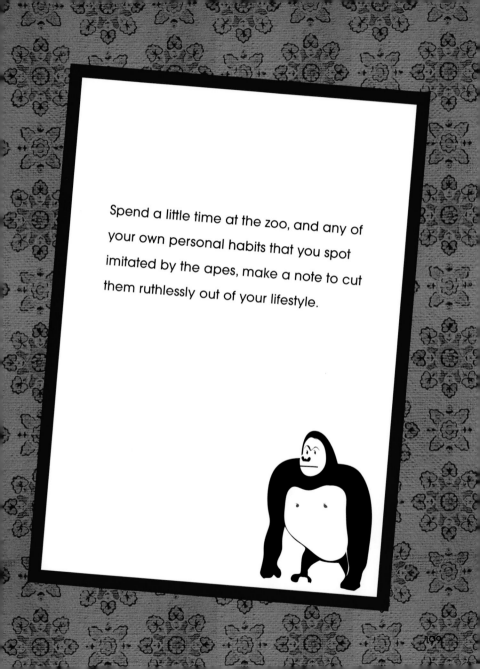

Dancing always conjures up painful images of gawky pubescence. Rock 'n' roll may have freed us from the awkward social maneuvers of yesteryear, but it doomed us to a half-century (and counting) of dance-floor twitching.

"Which extremity shall I launch about, or which part of my body should I shake to no beat in particular?" So inelegant. Do I dare suggest dancing lessons?

Men pose. Big-chested, bow-legged, staunchly virile, alpha males have always demonstrated their sexual prowess by the way they walk, talk, and sit.

There is, however, a time and a place. Any other attempt to demonstrate your sexual prowess in public would get you arrested. There's a thin line between "cool" and "sexual predator."

Try to avoid pouting and fixing people with your "steely" gaze. And if you ever feel the need to sashay in public, kick a nearby lamppost or fire hydrant. The resulting limp should keep your swagger in hand.

BODYBUILDING POSER

Do you remember our little lessons about subtlety? Here's another area in which to apply them.

If you are lucky enough to have developed a musculature worth displaying, think carefully about the manner in which you display it.

Some manly displays come closer to acts of self-love than legitimate invitations for the admiration of others.

Wearing lifting gloves outside the gym is one of these. Gratuitously holding your arms at a flattering angle is another.

Never, ever kiss your own bicep in public.

Scratching an itch is one of the primal urges that evolution has failed to quell. However, in this suspiciously hygienic day and age, society cruelly assumes the worst about any man tending to an itch in an intimate area.

If you're caught scratching in the vicinity of the buttocks, for instance, people might mistakenly think you're suffering from hemorrhoids, or worse, some kind of tapeworm.

If you're caught scratching near your crotch, people might begin to wonder what, exactly, you have going on down there, which in this particular scenario is not a good thing.

What can you do when the nether regions demand a little attention? Discreet squirming is permitted. Any further action requires the privacy of a locked room or toilet cubicle.

If neither is available, the itch much be heroically ignored. Concentrate hard on something else— your oracle prefers the thought of a distant beach. Biting your tongue can also help distract you from the pain.

The first draft of the Ten Commandments included "Thou shalt not pick thy nose." It got left out in favor of graven idols, but nose-picking should still be regarded as a mortal sin.

What exactly do you expect to find up there? A mineral seam? Relics of an ancient civilization? The thought makes me want to stop shaking people's hands altogether.

An epidemiologist has calculated that the influenza pandemic of 1918–19 was so widespread because of the common habit of shaking hands.

I suddenly feel like I might need a pair of latex gloves with me at all times. In the meantime, where's my hand-sanitizer?

There's nothing like a public display of contempt for your fellow creatures. Something about the male ego seems to revel in confrontation. But whatever it is that's got your goat, do try and suppress the urge to respond, especially if there are children present.

Why is it that good manners and good upbringing fly out the window with the first empty bottle? No matter how many drinks you've had, it is never acceptable to allow your hands to "wander" uninvited over an attractive stranger. Even if he or she is doing something as outrageously flirtatious as looking at you.

Anonymity, busy crowds, and the cover of a hectic transport system may also lead you to believe that a quick fondle is permissible. A word of advice: giving in to this urge may just lead to you being felt up yourself—in a jail cell.

A few further key points for playing with others:

Engage an attractive girl eye to eye, not eye to breast.

Attempt a few gentlemanly manners, such as opening doors for ladies or offering your partner your arm.

On no account use a "line." Women are secretly trained during adolescence to spot them, and instantly ridicule anybody attempting to use one.

CONCLUSiON

I hope you have enjoyed our tour through this fashion house of horrors. I trust for your sakes that it hasn't been a hall of mirrors.

If the pitfalls here highlighted and the advice here given seem obvious to you, then you may count yourself a blessed paragon of sartorial virtue. Congratulations. Have a cookie. Then, consider the plight of your less fortunate brethren, and perhaps pass a copy of this book to them with a light-hearted slap on the back and the relevant page tactfully marked. They will thank you for it in the fullness of time—or failing that, their nearest and dearest will.

If, however, you do recognize in these pages even the merest shadow of yourself, take a moment to consider the effect it may have on others and the steps you might take to alleviate their suffering. If a single one of you trims a ponytail or removes a sock from 'neath his sandal after reading this, I shall count my work well done.

All that said, of course, individual style must still have its place. If you are determined to wear a feather boa and top hat, there is nothing I or anyone else can or should do to stop you. The aim of dressing fashionably is to feel good about oneself, and any strictures that fail to accomplish this are not worth the paper on which they're printed.

So adieu, my friends, and remember: walk softly, and always carry a pair of clippers.

P.S. Actually, I'd pass on the feather boa. I really would.